DINOSAURS RULED!

TRICERATOPS

LEIGH ROCKWOOD

PowerKiDS press
New York

Published in 2012 by The Rosen Publishing Group, Inc.
29 East 21st Street, New York, NY 10010

First Edition

Editor: Joanne Randolph
Book Design: Kate Laczynski

Photo Credits: Cover, title page by Brian Garvey; cover background (palm tree leaves) © www.iStockphoto.com/dra_schwartz; cover background (palm tree trunk) iStockphoto/Thinkstock; cover background (ginkgo leaves) Hemera/Thinkstock; cover background (fern leaves) Brand X Pictures/Thinkstock; cover background (moss texture) © www.iStockphoto.com/Robert Linton; pp. 4, 5, 6, 8, 9, 10, 11, 12–13, 14, 15, 16, 18–19 © 2011 Orpheus Books Ltd.; p. 7 © www.iStockphoto.com/Beboy_ltd; p. 17 © www.iStockphoto.com/Ekely; p. 20 © www.iStockphoto.com/David Parsons; p. 21 Louie Psihoyos/Getty Images; p. 22 © www.iStockphoto.com/Josh Laverty.

Library of Congress Cataloging-in-Publication Data

Rockwood, Leigh.
  Triceratops / by Leigh Rockwood. — 1st ed.
    p. cm. — (Dinosaurs ruled!)
  Includes index.
  ISBN 978-1-4488-4969-7 (library binding) — ISBN 978-1-4488-5088-4 (pbk.) —
ISBN 978-1-4488-5089-1 (6-pack)
  1. Triceratops—Juvenile literature. I. Title.
  QE862.O65R6254 2012
  567.915'8—dc22
                                    2011000100

Manufactured in the United States of America

CPSIA Compliance Information: Batch #WS11PK: For Further Information contact Rosen Publishing, New York, New York at 1-800-237-9932

CONTENTS

MEET THE TRICERATOPS

The triceratops is the largest and the most famous of a group of dinosaurs called ceratopsian, or horned-faced, dinosaurs. "Triceratops" means "three-horned face." Along with the three horns on its face, the triceratops had a bony collar, or frill, around the back of its head.

Plant-eating dinosaurs, such as the triceratops, were an important source of food for meat-eating dinosaurs, such as the T. rex.

The triceratops is known for its three horns and bony plate, called a frill, on its head.

When **paleontologists** dig up triceratops **fossils**, they hope to find new clues about these dinosaurs. They come up with new theories, or ideas, based on the information they get from the fossils. This is how scientists learn about animals that have been **extinct** for millions of years.

THE LATE CRETACEOUS PERIOD

Earth's history goes back billions of years. Scientists use a system called geologic time to break this down into smaller historical periods. The triceratops lived at the very end of the Late Cretaceous period. This period lasted from 89 to 65 million years ago.

Meat eaters, such as the T. rex, were happy to make a meal out of a triceratops. The triceratops may have tried to fight back, but it was likely no match for a T. rex.

There was a great deal of volcanic activity during prehistoric times. Scientists think one possible cause of the dinosaurs' extinction was a big eruption.

Plant life was plentiful during the Late Cretaceous period. This meant there was plenty of food for a plant-eating dinosaur like the triceratops. Unfortunately for the triceratops, there were also many kinds of meat-eating dinosaurs, such as the T. rex, that **preyed** on plant-eating dinosaurs! Dinosaurs became extinct at the end of the Late Cretaceous period.

WHERE DID THE TRICERATOPS LIVE?

The triceratops lived in what are today the U.S. states of Wyoming, South Dakota, Montana, and Colorado. It also lived in the Canadian provinces of Alberta and Saskatchewan. The Rocky Mountains run through these areas and have lots of **sedimentary rocks** in them. These are the kind of rock in which fossils are found.

The triceratops lived in a habitat with lots of plants and other animals. The weather might have been like that of tropical places today.

During the Late Cretaceous period, the lands where the triceratops lived were thickly forested. The **climate** had been warm and humid but was beginning to cool as the sea in the middle of North America dried up. Dinosaurs living at the same time as the triceratops included not only the T. rex, but also the armored dinosaur ankylosaurus.

The triceratops shared watering holes and feeding places with other dinosaurs, such as the ankylosaurus.

THE TRICERATOPS'S BODY

The triceratops was the biggest and heaviest of all the ceratopsian dinosaurs. An adult triceratops was about 30 feet (9 m) long, 10 feet (3 m) tall, and weighed 5 tons (4.5 t). The triceratops's head was about 10 feet (3 m) long. The brain inside its big head was fairly small, though. Paleontologists think the

This plant-eating dinosaur munched on ferns and other low-lying plants using its beaklike mouth and cheek teeth.

DINO BITE

The ceratopsians included more than 30 different kinds of horned-faced dinosaurs. Each kind had a different frill shape and number of face horns. Do you see the differences between this styracosaurus and the triceratops?

triceratops's brain was about the size of a person's fist. Neither the triceratops's senses nor intelligence were likely very sharp.

The triceratops had four thick, strong legs. Paleontologists do not think it could move very quickly because of its weight and shape. Luckily, plants do not need to be chased!

A THREE-HORNED DINOSAUR

Like other ceratopsians, the triceratops had horns on its face. The triceratops had one short horn on its nose and a longer horn above each eye. The horns as you might see them on a skeleton in a museum show only the part of the horns that were made of bone. The bones were also covered in a layer of a material called keratin, though. Keratin is the same material that makes up your fingernails.

The triceratops with the strongest, sharpest horns would have been the winner of more mates. It also would have been able to fight off more predators.

The triceratops's horns gave the dinosaur some **protection** against **predators**. These horns were also likely used to draw **mates**. Males may have used their horns to fight other males for mates, as do today's deer.

DINO BITE

With its keratin covering, the triceratops's horns may have been 40 percent larger than the skeletal remains we see today. That is a lot bigger!

WHAT A FRILL!

DINO BITE

The triceratops's frill may have been a way for dinosaurs to identify one another.

The triceratops had a bony frill on the back of its head. Paleontologists once thought that the frill helped protect the dinosaur's neck. As they studied more fossils, though, scientists' ideas changed. They realized that the frill was unlikely to stop predators like the T. rex.

The triceratops's frill was about 6 feet (2 m) wide. It may have been brightly colored to draw mates.

Paleontologists now think that for a large predator like the T. rex, the triceratops's frill would not pose much of a problem.

Paleontologists came up with new theories about the frill. They think males may have used their frills to draw mates. Thick skin covered the frill, so it may have helped the triceratops keep from getting too hot or cold, too. It could let out body heat during hot weather or help the dinosaur warm up in the sun on cool days.

A PLANT-EATING DINOSAUR

Do you see how the triceratops's pointed mouth looks like a bird's beak? The triceratops used its hard beak to break off twigs and other plant matter.

The triceratops was an **herbivore**, or a plant eater. It ate many kinds of plants, such as ferns and cycads, which were plentiful in the Late Cretaceous period.

The triceratops used its parrotlike beak to break off bits of low-lying plants. Then its teeth ground the plant matter into tiny pieces. The food likely **fermented** in its gut, which is how animals like today's cows break down food. The fermentation helps get the most **nutrients** possible out of the food. This is important for a big animal that eats lots of low-nutrient plants.

The triceratops lived in places that had plenty of plants, such as ferns like these shown here. They would have needed to eat a lot of plants to fuel their large bodies!

IN THE HERD

Paleontologists think that triceratopses lived in herds. They think this because they have found groups of triceratops fossils together. The scientists' theory is that if a group of animals died together at the same time, they likely lived as a group, too.

Paleontologists have also found groupings of

Here a triceratops herd walks together looking for food. This is a common way for plant eaters today to keep themselves safe, too.

triceratops tracks. In these groupings, the smaller tracks of young dinosaurs are in the middle and the larger tracks of adults are on the outside. This suggests that the herd would protect its young from predators as the herd traveled.

DINO BITE

Groups of fossils that are found in the same place are sometimes called dinosaur graveyards.

NO FOSSIL GOES TO WASTE!

DINO BITE

Paleontologists knew that the T. rex likely preyed on the triceratops when they found pieces of its bones in a T. rex coprolite.

Paleontologists have studied the fossils of many kinds of ceratopsians of different ages. They have found that horns and frills were very small on young ceratopsians and reached their full size only on adult dinosaurs. This suggested to scientists that the horns and frills in dinosaurs like the triceratops were more for show than for protection.

These fossilized triceratops footprints were found in Golden, Colorado. They give scientists information about how fast a dinosaur moved and whether it traveled in groups.

This paleontologist is studying dinosaur tracks that were found in the Alps in Italy.

Bones are not the only parts of dinosaurs that become fossilized. Paleontologists have found not only fossilized dinosaur eggs and footprints, but also fossilized waste, or **coprolites**. It sounds gross, but scientists use coprolites to find clues about what a dinosaur ate.

NO BONES ABOUT IT

The first museum to have a triceratops **exhibit** was the Smithsonian Institution National Museum of Natural History. Their exhibit was built in 1905 from bones that came from many triceratopses. This meant that some of the bones were the wrong size for the skeleton in the exhibit.

Although many bones have been dug up, no complete triceratops skeleton has yet been found.

When the Smithsonian's exhibit was taken apart to be cleaned and repaired, scientists took pictures of the dinosaur's bones. Then they used the pictures to make a computer model of the triceratops. They resized the pictures of bones and made **casts** to replace bones that were the wrong size. This gave paleontologists a better understanding of an animal that had been extinct for 65 million years.

GLOSSARY

casts (KASTS) Objects made by pouring something into molds and letting it harden.

climate (KLY-mit) The kind of weather a certain place has.

coprolites (KO-pruh-lyts) Fossilized waste.

exhibit (ig-ZIH-bit) A public show.

extinct (ik-STINGKT) No longer existing.

fermented (fer-MENT-ed) Changed in a way that makes gas bubbles.

fossils (FO-sulz) The hardened remains of dead animals or plants.

herbivore (ER-buh-vor) An animal that eats only plants.

mates (MAYTS) Partners for making babies.

nutrients (NOO-tree-unts) Food that a living thing needs to live and grow.

paleontologists (pay-lee-on-TAH-luh-jists) People who study things that lived in the past.

predators (PREH-duh-terz) Animals that kill other animals for food.

preyed (PRAYD) Hunted for food.

protection (pruh-TEK-shun) Something that keeps something else from being hurt.

sedimentary rocks (seh-deh-MEN-teh-ree ROKS) Stones, sand, or mud that has been pressed together to form rock.

INDEX

WEB SITES

Due to the changing nature of Internet links, PowerKids Press has developed an online list of Web sites related to the subject of this book. This site is updated regularly. Please use this link to access the list:

www.powerkidslinks.com/dinr/trice/

0 ML   11 /11